Tales of My Thoughts

Tales of My Thoughts

AMTI KAMARA

RESOURCE *Publications* • Eugene, Oregon

TALES OF MY THOUGHTS

Resource Publications
An Imprint of Wipf and Stock Publishers
199 W. 8th Ave., Suite 3
Eugene, OR 97401

www.wipfandstock.com

PAPERBACK ISBN: 978-1-7252-5814-3
HARDCOVER ISBN: 978-1-7252-5815-0
EBOOK ISBN: 978-1-7252-5816-7

Manufactured in the U.S.A.   12/23/19

I dedicate this collection to anyone who needs it. Have faith and take the leap. No one except you can stop you. Love yourself.

I see, I write
I feel, I write
I just love it

Contents

THE MARK OF MY EXISTENCE

A name was given to me
A choice made by my caretaker

Forcefully I wore it with pride
my consent was not required

The name is now my brand
Without the name, there is no me

A name is my curse
that is bound to ache

The first impression of me
is my name without a face

A name might be my escape
but a name is my life

A name tells not my story
but a name is me

A name was given to me
without a name, there is no me

FACE = 2

Is my face pretty?
Is my face ugly?
I look in the mirror,
All I see is a reflection.

It smiles though there is nothing to be happy about.
It laughs though there is nothing funny being said.
It´s fake,
It is a mask.

So, what is my real face?
Is it what I see in the mirror
Or is it what I feel?
I don´t know.

I can´t tell the difference.
The face is scarred.
Why does one smile,
While the other stays emotionless?

Damn it, it is my face.
I should know, right?
But hell no!
I am just a mask.

FEAR OF FAILURE

The Want to improve keeps me up all night
The fading motivation gains its sparks
As doubt doubles in size
Fear of failure battles it out
with the slowing growing faith to succeed

A guitar reminds me of a lost dream
One that was to be obtained
The efforts I thrust were futile
Now the strings of guitar play
the victory song of my failure

Pictures on TV show me my unfeigned wish
My mind is divided as my body waits for a command
But my determination fails.
Now, the strings are replaying
their song of my failure.

TRAGEDY TO MY YOUTH

Sleeping till noon
No thoughts of waking up

Dreaming big
But no realization effort

Waste of thoughts
Waste of time
Youth is just a spark, my dear

Dreaming is for the night
Reality comes with the morning
Youth is not forever, sweet child

State of emptiness, I find myself
With the want to move
But the big push is absent

Wasted years are yet to come
I am scared
What a tragedy to my Youth

NO ONE CARES

I fell down the stairs
I hurt my leg
But I lived alone
there was no one to tell

I limped to work
I was late
And my boss was angry
Real-life is the stage

I was slow
I was trying
But no one cares
For I am a grown-up

I was in pain
I was alone
My mom´s words resurfaced
You are a big girl now

BEING SAMANTHA JONES

I was aiming to be a Samantha Jones
by the age of 23. Hmpf
But I am still a teen
Without the usual tantrums.
People have expectations but I too
Am wise to have mines, luckily.
My goal was to be fucking happy
And owning it.
But my state of mind wavers
Even by the smallest turbulence.
I am opened but closed,
In the present yet in the past;
In the future too, somehow.
I am all over the place, lol
But I should be focusing in the seconds of now
I was aiming for Samantha Jones´s lifestyle
By the age of 23
What was I thinking?

PICTURE ON THE WALL

There is a picture hanging on the wall. - It is slightly slanted I think, but then again it might be completely bent – Hold up! Maybe, just maybe, I am slightly slanted or even bent – Hmm, whatever I don´t know. Is something wrong with my vision? –

This brings up a thought, how do my classmates see it? – Do they see it slightly slant or completely bent? – I can´t ask, can I? –

But then again, I think I am the only one being bothered by it. – Now, I ask myself again – "Am I too different? Am I too critical? – or am I too idly?" Well, I think my vision is just different from others. –

WHERE ARE MY EMOTIONS?

I don´t like the internet.

One minute you are reading a sad article,

The next you are laughing to a GoT´s memes,

Moaning over the latest abs of Zac Efron

And questioning yourself about the tendencies of
humans.

The internet is a rollercoaster

And my emotions are never stable.

But I love its platforms.

They keep me entertained.

Nothing affects me longer than five seconds, max.

And I am addicted to these shallow feelings.

I don´t resent deep impactful emotions.

But I do have to say they are tormenting,

Oh my goodness, I am turning into a deadpan.

No, I want my emotions back.

MY FIRST TIME FIGHTING BACK

When the snow left the ground
and the choirs were singing
I fought back
I was infuriated
by the barking sound called voice
But their one-sided need
their nagging was unwarranted
their act was petty
and I couldn´t stand it
I snapped
I screamed and screamed
but my words took no effect
then something broke in me
and I lost my sight, my hearing
and sadly, my control too
As I regained my senses
something shiny was in my grasp
a tiny shimmer
I panicked and ran
what is becoming of me?
I snapped that wasn´t me
fear swallowed me in one piece.
Am I still me? I wondered
How many sides are there to me?
I fought back but now
fear of self has manifested

MEMORIES

People come and go,
But their memories stay.
Be it happy or sad,
It´s part of you now, embrace it.

Time flows and changes,
But the pain stays.
Don´t be delusional,
Time doesn´t heal it, replay it.

It plays, replays and plays,
The memories are changing.
Pain and Joy are blending in,
Finally, we are owning it.

A BITTER CUP OF TEA

My treasure, my heart
not stable but yet
presents in its glory of red
My focus is wavering
no topic, just blank

My mind is riding a train
all while being intoxicated
by words and emotions
I wish to shake off
I am not at ease

I long for many but
I must be lacking
not in determination
but what it takes
so, it seems

I dare not say more
For I don´t know
what I know
my heart is filled
with loathing and pain

I can´t rid myself
of the angry and humiliation
my guards were down
it hurts because
the source was a friend, I trusted

Pain and hatred
I want to escape
to ease and lose the weight
cold is not my shade
my heart is not your Chest

NOT MINE

My skin is crawling,
Goosebumps are trendy.
But the weather is not the supplier.
The windows are closed,
I am sitting on a Jensen,
Within a wall of four
And a pyramid to boot.
But none is mine.
My host is on the phone.
His mom can´t know,
I am here, I am not his.
But his words are my command.
I was invited.
I asked for a favor.
I am being too loud, he said.
Not home, this is.

OUR WALK

As we, five, stroll
under the light
Of the stars.
Each with pains of our own
buried in the depth of
our weaken yet strong heart.
Our pains slowly ease
But it will never be gone.
The sound of our laughter
blessed our hurtful souls.

DON´T GIVE UP

I didn´t fail,
I just didn´t make it.

I wasn´t good enough,
But I am good enough to try again.

SOFT AS METAL

Soft as metal
Your words can´t enter
I stand by my words
Though they are wrong

Stupid as I may be
But that´s just me
The embarrassment I bring
I will endure its sting

Time will pass by
And I will climb high
For the work is hard
I will plow yards

My words are wrong
But my heart is strong
I will face the devil
For I am soft as metal

ALL IS WELL

No mistakes allowed
The clock is ticking
Though you fell back
All is still well

You lost your track
With abundant feeling
You crawled back in
And all is still well

You live, you die
With seconds approaching
You crush down
And all is still well

You moved, you fell
Insecurities are emerging
You snuck back in
And all is still well

One step forward
And three steps back
You buried yourself
And all is still well

Struggles and Persuasions
The pain intensified
You held yourself
And all is still well

Breathe, breathe
Breathe, breathe
And again breathe
And all is still well.

TRUST IN THYSELF

All that you love
is all that you need
you can have it all
but you have to believe

So, trust in yourself
you know what´s best
trust in yourself
and you can have it all

WHEN WILL I HAVE A BREAK?

I die every time I see myself.
My eyes are sad but
The reasons are known.
I cry every time I hear myself speak.
For my words counter my truth.
Round and round, I go
In a circle, I never stop.
My feet are numb,
And my heart is cold.
When will I get a break?

My hands are sore.
"I am sorry," these words
I have written thousands of times.
"I didn´t mean to,"
This too has lost its meaning.
Everything now is brittle.
No depth, just crumbling shells
My tears have dried up,
And my toes are frozen.
When will I have a break?

MY COAT

I have nothing on my plate
my hands are aching
but I have money on my brain

I carry the blame
bills are meant to be paid
I have too many desires

I work, worked and work
still, I stand at the edge
I have taken life too far

I walk in my labyrinth of life
with a hunger for more
but I hope to be content, someday

BLACK FRIDAY

Auch, my feet hurt
43 shops and no bags
my heart is breaking
I want to be rich
I have said it
I am materialistic, so what?
try living when
a daily strawberry frappuccino
is the new norm
I am done with cutting down
I want to live
while affording the basis
that Gucci dress, those red bottoms
those silver bling around my neck
those tears-drop earrings
oh goodness, my ears will bleed
but who cares?
I want to drown myself
in black Friday
shopping is the new air.

HALLOWEEN

Witches on brooms,
Vampires on beer diet.
The world is crazy
And candy rules the mind.
It is Halloween!
So, suck up your fears
And live out the worst.
Cheers to the Underworld!

SPRING IS HERE

The raindrops are falling
Flowers are blooming
The earth smells fresh
And my nose is tingly
Jackets are out
Fresh skin is the trend
Dressed in shorts
I am not searching
But yet

Hot drinks are bitter
But juices are sweeter
Ice creams are creamy
But scales are tricksters
Sceneries are striking
But I am prettier
Here we go again
It is beginning
But yet

Grasses are greener
But footsteps are killers
Ponds are cleaner
But noses are bleeders
People are hoping
It´s the season of love
Spring is here
And I am searching
And yet

"Why am I single?"

WHEN LOVE COMES, LOVE WILL COME

When love appears,
the feeling of excitement cannot be measured.
When love arrives, aging stops,
time stands still as the heart rate increases.
The unexpected guest that brings its rollercoaster,
I expect more and less from its coming.
The excitement of unforeseeable joy
whispers its happy deductions
And my mind is blinded by its wishful thinking.
With these thoughts the night becomes endless,
but I can´t stop smiling at the thought of your coming.
This endless battle freezes my heart,
but I stay afloat as I see your face.
That hearten smiles you sent,
keeps my hope up that you will surely come,
On a day less expected.

THE HATE GAME, THE LOVE GAME

I used to celebrate this fluffy feeling building up in my
heart.
But I got burned, third degree, my friend.
That fluffy feeling is back.
And I have to play this game I hate,
The game I hate.

"I like you" was his first words.
But all I can remember is his lasts
"I can´t stand you"
And it was a matter of nights, four nights to be exact.
Feelings change so easily, scary hmm.

Every time, this fluffy feeling returns,
I resist with all my might.
But at the end of the day,
 I just embrace it
And join in the game.

I am not complaining, don´t get me wrong.
The game is intense, exciting, fresh, fun.
But I hate I have to play it
But I play the game I hate
Because my heart always yields,
So, I play the game I hate to play
Hmm, love.

YES AND NO

I have lots of love to give,
I believe.
But, no one is there to receive
I think.
I tried not to be strict,
but I have standards.

I have tried to do it right.
But all the time, it seems wrong.
Am I too much?
Or am I too cold?
There is a flame within my heart
masked by a layer of ice.

In the season of my winter,
I long for a spring.
Hot and cold, my heart is on fire.
Hot and cold, I never let them in.
Hot and Cold,
I am not ready for spring.

PAN, PAN, PAN

A human touch,
Skin on skin
Causes a flood of butterflies.
But my story as it is
Is a sad and painful one.

A flood of butterflies
Doesn´t occur at my will.
Moments of sparks happen
Like waterfalls for others.
I assume.

But I am left unmoved.
But when it does occur,
It wavers from person to person.
Leaving me questioning
my very own being.

But at my current age
And confidence to boot,
I finally opened my eyes,
Undo my mask and
Face my truth.

I have embraced it
And promised to live for me.
For I, by the name given to me,
Love my P-self
And promise to love.

THE DREAMER I AM

Where would you be
when the light goes off?
I will be in my corner
dreaming of stories
I wish to tell

I do not possess hardcore facts
But I am in possession
of a mystical artifact
My imagination will suffice
for all the lacks I bear

My life is blessed by the passion
to strive in this chosen path
The future is not visible
for my inexperienced eyes
but I trust my instinct

Fate will take me
along on the ride
of this quest of joy
I trust in the will
of the dreamer in me

THE IMPERFECT ME

When I was 17
Everyone had a crush
Some liked celebrities
Others the new kid in town
And then there was me
I liked anime guys
I was very unique

When I was 19
Sex was the topic
Some did it out of curiosity
Some were encouraged by puppy love
And then there was me
I was waiting for Edward
I was being foolish

When I was 21
the talk about the future was the It
Some took on internships
Some were learning new skills
and then there was me
I was yielding for the end of college
I was hanging on

When I was 22
going abroad was the trend
Some went East and discovered
Some went West and learned
And then there was me
I was indulging in excessive parties
I was living in the present

Now I am 24 years old
Work and Life are the dos
Some are starting a new job
Others are back in college
And there is me
I am chasing a dream
I am on my way

My clouded mind wanders around
Time will be the judge
if this state of mind is just
I view others with envy
for they are stable
while I am investing
But I am not complaining

I am walking on my path
while taking detours
but I carry their badges with me
As I am creating what I call
the best me
I am imperfect and slow
but surely, I will be fine

ME ON MY PATH

Have you ever felt lonely,
Caught listening to the beat of your heart?
Reminded of who you are
And that happiness isn't in your stars.

Have you ever felt lonely,
Caught listening to the voice in your head?
That tells you who you're meant to be
That success isn't yours to have.

Have you ever felt lonely,
Dreaming of who you can be?
But reminded of your flaws
But there is passion in your heart.

Have you ever felt lonely,
On the path, to who you are?
With no friends but a broken heart
But the sky is head up high.

Have I ever felt lonely,
Caught listening to the beat of my heart?
Reminded of who I truly am
And that happiness is mine to have.

FAREWELL, JELLI

Today a friend said goodbye
She was a warrior angel
She struggled every day
Her environment was toxic
with their unwarranted verbal poison
Bravery, she faced it daily,
but our warrior angel lost her wings
with her fall, she was gone

Today a stranger said goodbye
The news came in the morning
We know her songs
We knew her struggles,
but we were deceived by her smile
She was a singing angel,
but now she will sing with the angels,
this I said to myself

I didn´t know her pain,
and I couldn´t console her
when she was blue
So, sleep well, our fallen Angel
we will sing tunes of your bravery
Though this might come too late
in the name of your fans, I say
braless angel, you did well!

www.ingramcontent.com/pod-product-compliance
Lightning Source LLC
Chambersburg PA
CBHW051050030426
42339CB00006B/281